THIS BOOK BELONGS TO:

_____

_____

D0711819

QUESTION *of the* DAY

FOR COUPLES

HARVEST HOUSE PUBLISHERS
EUGENE, OREGON

INTRODUCTION

We've been married for more than 35 years, and while it's mostly been LOL, there have been some LULL times as well. And for those, it would have been great to have a book like this one.

This book's questions cover a wide array of topics and themes. Some of them will be simple to answer; some will take more thought. As each year unfolds, you will encounter some similar questions from month to month. This is by design, as it will let you see how you're changing and growing as individuals and as a couple through the months and years.

We've raised our own children and are now busy ~~spoiling~~ being firm but fair examples to our grandchildren, but we're still learning about each other. Whether you've been together 35 years or 35 minutes, there are always things to discover, to share, and to bring you closer to each other and to God.

Dan and Lana Taylor

Think about last year. What made you smile?

20___

20___

20___

"A cheerful heart is good medicine." —PROVERBS 17:22

What's something you have never done but would like to try?

20__ _____

_____

_____

_____

20__ _____

_____

_____

_____

20__ _____

_____

_____

_____

Thank you for the opportunities that surround us, Lord.
Help us discern them with wisdom and courage.

Change can be scary! But this question isn't: What's something you'd like to change about your morning routine?

20___

_____

_____

_____

_____

20___

_____

_____

_____

_____

20___

_____

_____

_____

_____

"Satisfy us in the morning with your unfailing love, that we may sing for joy and be glad all our days." PSALM 90:14

What is one thing your faith community does well?

20___

20___

20___

Lord, thank you for the abilities our faith community shares.

What do you think your faith community
(yourself included) could do better?

20___

_____

_____

_____

_____

20___

_____

_____

_____

_____

20___

_____

_____

_____

_____

Lord, give us eyes to see the needs around us.

What radio station do you like to play in the
car? Sports? News? Talk? Music?

20___ _____

20___ _____

20___ _____

What's one thing you would like to tell
every young person you know?

20___

20___

20___

"The foolishness of God is wiser than human wisdom, and the weakness of
God is stronger than human strength." —1 CORINTHIANS 1:25

If you could become fluent in another
language, what would it be?

20_ _ _____

_____

_____

_____

20_ _ _____

_____

_____

_____

20_ _ _____

_____

_____

_____

Lord, sweeten our words; please let them be full of grace.

You get to have dinner with anyone from history. Whom would you pick?

20___

20___

20___

Lord, give us a teachable spirit and wise mentors.

JANUARY 10

I wonder how...

20___

20___

20___

I wonder why...

20___

20___

20___

Lord, help us trust you in everything we don't understand.

You're at a wedding. Would you rather give a
toast or dance like everyone's watching?

20___ _____

_____

_____

_____

20___ _____

_____

_____

_____

20___ _____

_____

_____

_____

"Wearing a linen ephod, David was dancing before
the LORD with all his might." —2 SAMUEL 6:14

What is your favorite way to relax?

20___ _____

_____

_____

_____

20___ _____

_____

_____

_____

20___ _____

_____

_____

_____

"God blessed the seventh day and made it holy, because on it he rested
from all the work of creating that he had done." —GENESIS 2:3

My life would be easier if someone would invent...

20___ _____

_____

_____

_____

20___ _____

_____

_____

_____

20___ _____

_____

_____

_____

_____

Lord, thank you for the challenges each day
brings. Help us learn from them.

Mountains, beach, or big city—which would you choose today?

20_ _

20_ _

20_ _

We're grateful for your creation, Lord.

Who is your favorite disciple of Jesus?

20___

_____

_____

_____

_____

20___

_____

_____

_____

_____

20___

_____

_____

_____

_____

"Go and make disciples of all nations, baptizing them in the name of
the Father and of the Son and of the Holy Spirit." —MATTHEW 28:19

When it's cold outside, I like to...

20_ _ _____

_____

_____

_____

20_ _ _____

_____

_____

_____

20_ _ _____

_____

_____

_____

_____

Lord, thank you for the warmth and security of home.

What would you never in a million years buy online?

20___

_____

_____

_____

_____

20___

_____

_____

_____

_____

20___

_____

_____

_____

_____

_____

Dear God, please help us faithfully steward the blessings we have.

JANUARY 19

What's one trait you've noticed in each other
that you'd like to see blossom even more?

20___ _____

_____

_____

_____

20___ _____

_____

_____

_____

20___ _____

_____

_____

_____

"In days to come Jacob will take root, Israel will bud and
blossom and fill all the world with fruit." —ISAIAH 27:6

Who or what has challenged your thinking in the past year?

20__ _____

_____

_____

_____

20__ _____

_____

_____

_____

20__ _____

_____

_____

_____

_____

*Lord, as we face new inventions, ideas, and
thoughts, help us seek your wisdom.*

What's something you see differently
now compared to a year ago?

20___

20___

20___

The world changes, but you don't, Lord. Give us grace as we grow.

Among all our friends and relatives, the
marriage I admire the most is...

20___ _____

_____

_____

_____

20___ _____

_____

_____

_____

20___ _____

_____

_____

_____

Lord, please bless our relationship.

What's your favorite picture of yourself
currently? Why is it your favorite?

20___

20___

20___

"Your beauty should not come from outward adornment...Rather, it
should be that of your inner self, the unfading beauty of a gentle and
quiet spirit, which is of great worth in God's sight." —1 PETER 3:3-4

It's 3:00 in the morning, and you can't
sleep. What's keeping you up?

20___ _____

_____

_____

_____

20___ _____

_____

_____

_____

20___ _____

_____

_____

_____

In this turbulent world, give us peace that passes understanding.

By this time next year, I'm going to be
disappointed if I haven't...

20___ _____

_____

_____

_____

20___ _____

_____

_____

_____

20___ _____

_____

_____

_____

Lord, help us avoid measuring ourselves by worldly standards.

What part of being a year older makes you happy?

20__ _____

_____

_____

_____

20__ _____

_____

_____

_____

20__ _____

_____

_____

_____

"Gray hair is a crown of splendor; it is attained in the
way of righteousness." —PROVERBS 16:31

What part of being a year older makes you less than happy?

20___

20___

20___

Lord, we want to age gracefully. Give us insight on how to do that.

Think about your circle of friends. Who inspires you?
Who wears you out? Who makes you laugh?

20___ _____

_____

_____

_____

20___ _____

_____

_____

_____

20___ _____

_____

_____

_____

Thank you for our friends. Help us be a joy to them.

Think about your extended family. Who inspires you? Who wears you out? Who makes you laugh?

20___

_____

_____

_____

_____

_____

20___

_____

_____

_____

_____

_____

20___

_____

_____

_____

_____

_____

I feel the most comfortable when I'm wearing my...

20__ _____

_____

_____

_____

20__ _____

_____

_____

_____

20__ _____

_____

_____

_____

_____

Lord, when we're stressed, when we're tired, when we're not ourselves, give us grace.

What do you imagine will be your biggest
challenge in the year ahead?

20___

_____

_____

_____

_____

20___

_____

_____

_____

_____

20___

_____

_____

_____

_____

"Consider it pure joy, my brothers and sisters, whenever you
face trials of many kinds, because you know that the testing
of your faith produces perseverance." —JAMES 1:2-3

"The fruit of the Spirit is love" (Galatians 5:22). How many different kinds of love can you think of?

20___ _____

_____

_____

_____

20___ _____

_____

_____

_____

20___ _____

_____

_____

_____

_____

Lord, thank you for the love that surrounds us.

FEBRUARY 2

What's something that made the two of you fall
in love? What *keeps* you falling in love?

20___ _____

_____

_____

_____

20___ _____

_____

_____

_____

20___ _____

_____

_____

_____

_____

"How beautiful you are and how pleasing, my love,
with your delights!" —SONG OF SONGS 7:6

Set aside some time to spend together. What
would each of you like to do?

20___ _____

_____

_____

_____

20___ _____

_____

_____

_____

20___ _____

_____

_____

_____

Lord, help us find ways to go even deeper in our relationship.

What do you appreciate most about each other?

20____

20____

20____

"Gracious words are a honeycomb, sweet to the soul
and healing to the bones." —PROVERBS 16:24

What's something one of you did today
that meant a lot to the other?

20___ _____

_____

_____

_____

_____

20___ _____

_____

_____

_____

_____

20___ _____

_____

_____

_____

_____

*Lord, give us wisdom to recognize opportunities to
serve—and the strength to perform them.*

What kind of gift would each of you most like to receive?

20___

20___

20___

Thank you for the things we have, Lord. Help us use
them generously and enjoy them gratefully.

How do you decide how much touching is
enough, and how much is just too much?

20__ _____

_____

_____

_____

_____

20__ _____

_____

_____

_____

_____

20__ _____

_____

_____

_____

_____

Lord, we thank you for each other.

What's something you would like to hire somebody
to do that you usually do yourself?

20__ _____

20__ _____

20__ _____

Lord, when we face challenges, help us avoid
stubbornness and instead be filled with grace.

What was the most difficult activity you had to do last week?

20___ _____

_____

_____

_____

20___ _____

_____

_____

_____

20___ _____

_____

_____

_____

"Who shall separate us from the love of Christ? Shall
trouble or hardship or persecution or famine or
nakedness or danger or sword?" —ROMANS 8:35

What was the most fun activity you got to do last week?

20___

20___

20___

Thank you for the gift of laughter, Lord.

What's something you truly admire in your grandparents?

20___

20___

20___

Lord, we thank you for our heritage of faith. Help us be good stewards of it.

You're going to have dinner at your favorite restaurant. What will you order?

20___

_____
_____
_____
_____

20___

_____
_____
_____
_____

20___

_____
_____
_____
_____

Heavenly Father, we thank you for our capacity to enjoy the blessings of food and fellowship.

FEBRUARY 13

You're planning a romantic dinner. What will you make?

20__ __

20__ __

20__ __

"Better a dry crust with peace and quiet than a house
full of feasting, with strife." —PROVERBS 17:1

What's a romantic gift that really says
"Happy Valentine's Day" to you?

20___ _____

_____

_____

_____

20___ _____

_____

_____

_____

20___ _____

_____

_____

_____

_____

Thank you for the gift of our love, Lord. Help us honor you with it.

How are you like your dad?

20____ _____

_____

_____

_____

20____ _____

_____

_____

_____

20____ _____

_____

_____

_____

_____

Thank you for the fathers in our lives. Help us reflect
their strength, courage, and steadfastness.

How are you like your mom?

20___

20___

20___

*Thank you for the mothers in our lives. Help us reflect
their tenderness, grace, and compassion.*

You may try to avoid or ignore it, but what's something you find annoying?

20___

20___

20___

What talents do your young children, nieces, nephews, or cousins have that surprise you?

20___

_____

_____

_____

_____

20___

_____

_____

_____

_____

20___

_____

_____

_____

_____

_____

Lord, children are such blessings. Thank you for placing them in our lives.

FEBRUARY 19

Who's at the top of your prayer list? How can you help?

20___

20___

20___

Father God, we come to you in humility, reverence,
and hope. Thank you for hearing us.

What three items would you say are truly worth the money?

20___

20___

20___

Lord, help us see through the materialism
that surrounds us and focus on you.

What three items would you say are
absolutely *not* worth the money?

20__ _____

_____

_____

_____

20__ _____

_____

_____

_____

20__ _____

_____

_____

_____

Thank you for the gift of discernment, Lord.

FEBRUARY 22

What's something that recently caused you
stress, but didn't end up being so bad?

20__ _____
_____
_____
_____

20__ _____
_____
_____
_____

20__ _____
_____
_____
_____

"We live by faith, not by sight." —2 CORINTHIANS 5:7

You're snowed in and the power's out. How
would you like to spend the evening?

20___

_____

_____

_____

_____

20___

_____

_____

_____

_____

20___

_____

_____

_____

_____

We have so many distractions. Lord, help us keep our eyes on you.

Which three qualities do you admire most in each other?

20__

20__

20__

Thank you for the gift of love.

What's something about the kids in your
life that always makes you smile?

20___

20___

20___

Lord, we thank you for the joy you bring into our lives through children.

What's something your younger self did that your
current self wouldn't even think about trying?

20__ _____

_____

_____

_____

_____

20__ _____

_____

_____

_____

_____

20__ _____

_____

_____

_____

_____

"Wisdom, like an inheritance, is a good thing and benefits
those who see the sun." —ECCLESIASTES 7:11

I feel most like an adult when I...

20___

20___

20___

Which day of the week is your favorite day?
If you were given an extra day, what would you love to do with it?

20___

20___

20___

"Can any one of you by worrying add a single hour to your life?" —MATTHEW 6:27

"The fruit of the Spirit is...joy" (Galatians 5:22). What's something you can do this week to put more joy into your relationship?

20___ _____

_____

_____

_____

20___ _____

_____

_____

_____

20___ _____

_____

_____

_____

_____

Lord, help us find something to be joyful about each day.

What's something the two of you can do
for someone else to bring them joy?

20___

20___

20___

"Do not grieve, for the joy of the LORD is your strength." —NEHEMIAH 8:10

MARCH 3

What current news story has made you happy?

20_ _ _____

_____

_____

_____

20_ _ _____

_____

_____

_____

20_ _ _____

_____

_____

_____

Thank you for the reasons we have to celebrate.

What current news story has made you anxious?

20___

20___

20___

Lord, give us a calm spirit when we're tempted to worry.

What was the most interesting discussion you
had with someone in the past week?

20___ _____

_____

_____

_____

_____

20___ _____

_____

_____

_____

_____

20___ _____

_____

_____

_____

_____

How have you seen the Spirit of God
working in your life recently?

20___

20___

20___

What are you looking forward to in the next few months?

20___ _____
_____
_____
_____

20___ _____
_____
_____
_____
_____

20___ _____
_____
_____
_____
_____

Lord, direct our plans and bless the paths we take.

What's one of your parents' (or mentor's)
most treasured memories?

20___

_____

_____

_____

_____

20___

_____

_____

_____

_____

20___

_____

_____

_____

_____

You've put some wonderful people in our lives, Lord. Thank you!

Where are you in the birth order of your family?
How is that playing out for you as an adult?

20__ _____

_____

_____

_____

20__ _____

_____

_____

_____

20__ _____

_____

_____

_____

_____

Lord, thank you for siblings and friends who are as close as siblings.

What aspect of your relationship keeps you awake at night?

20_ _

_____

_____

_____

_____

20_ _

_____

_____

_____

_____

20_ _

_____

_____

_____

_____

"Do not be anxious about anything, but in every
situation, by prayer and petition, with thanksgiving,
present your requests to God." —PHILIPPIANS 4:6

Whose marriage is teaching you something you want to avoid?

20___

_____

_____

_____

_____

20___

_____

_____

_____

_____

20___

_____

_____

_____

_____

Lord, please bless the spouses who are facing tough times.

What's one chore you could do for a loved one this week?

20___

20___

20___

If you two could swap talents with each
other, which ones would you pick?

20___

20___

20___

Are you more likely to try new items at a
restaurant or to stick with what you know?

20___

20___

20___

Lord, thank you for little adventures wherever they appear.

What's something you'd like to learn more about?

20___

_____

_____

_____

20___

_____

_____

_____

20___

_____

_____

_____

*Lord, we thank you for curiosity and the capacity
to keep growing and learning.*

Besides your significant other, who's
someone you *know* you can count on?

20__ _____
_____
_____
_____
_____

20__ _____
_____
_____
_____
_____

20__ _____
_____
_____
_____
_____

"Love does not delight in evil but rejoices with the truth. It always protects,
always trusts, always hopes, always perseveres." —1 CORINTHIANS 13:6-7

What's something you like about your
kids' (or a young relative's) friends?

20___ _____

_____

_____

_____

_____

20___ _____

_____

_____

_____

_____

20___ _____

_____

_____

_____

_____

Thank you for the fun surprises children bring into our lives.

MARCH 18

What's something that concerns you about
your kids' (or a young relative's) friends?

20___

20___

20___

*Dear God, give us discernment and wisdom when
it comes to the children in our lives.*

What's something guaranteed to improve your mood?

20___ _____

_____

_____

_____

_____

20___ _____

_____

_____

_____

20___ _____

_____

_____

_____

"His anger lasts only a moment, but his favor lasts a lifetime; weeping may stay for the night, but rejoicing comes in the morning." —PSALM 30:5

Right now, what do you find most attractive in each other?

20___ _____

_____

_____

_____

20___ _____

_____

_____

_____

20___ _____

_____

_____

_____

_____

Lord, thank you for the deepening and strengthening
of our relationship over time.

Think of a relative you'd gladly lend a serious
amount of money. What name comes to mind?

20___

_____

_____

_____

_____

20___

_____

_____

_____

_____

20___

_____

_____

_____

_____

Thank you for our families, Lord. Help us treat them fairly and well.

MARCH 22

Spring is in the air! What's a favorite spring memory?

20___

20___

20___

*As the earth again turns green with new
life, we give you thanks, our Creator.*

MARCH 23

What's changed about your walk with God?
Is it where you think it should be?

20___ _____

_____

_____

_____

_____

20___ _____

_____

_____

_____

20___ _____

_____

_____

_____

_____

"Follow God's example, therefore, as dearly loved children and walk
in the way of love, just as Christ loved us and gave himself up for
us as a fragrant offering and sacrifice to God." —EPHESIANS 5:1-2

MARCH 29

What would your dream birthday look like?

20___

20___

20___

"Methuselah lived a total of 969 years." —GENESIS 5:27

MARCH 25

What's something you feel you've done really well
when interacting with your kids or someone else's?
What's something you wish you had done better?

20___ _____

_____

_____

_____

20___ _____

_____

_____

_____

20___ _____

_____

_____

_____

_____

Thank you for the children in our lives, Lord.

Think about your parents' relationship.
What's something you admire?

20___ _____

_____

_____

_____

_____

20___ _____

_____

_____

_____

_____

20___ _____

_____

_____

_____

_____

*The examples we had growing up made us the people
we are today, and we thank you, Lord.*

What's something about your parents' relationship
that you don't want to emulate?

20___

_____

_____

_____

_____

20___

_____

_____

_____

_____

20___

_____

_____

_____

_____

*Help us forgive the mistakes that were made by our parents,
and please forgive the mistakes we have made as well.*

If you won a free one-room makeover,
which room would you choose?

20___

20___

20___

"Unless the LORD builds the house, the builders
labor in vain." —PSALM 127:1

Looking back over the past year, what's
something you're really proud of?

20____

20____

20____

MARCH 30

What's one piece of furniture you'd like to get rid of? What's one you want to keep forever?

20___

20___

20___

Tomorrow is April Fools' Day! Who has
a sense of humor you like?

20__ _____

_____

_____

_____

20__ _____

_____

_____

_____

20__ _____

_____

_____

_____

"He will yet fill your mouth with laughter and
your lips with shouts of joy." —JOB 8:21

"The fruit of the Spirit is...peace" (Galatians 5:22). What's something in your relationship that gives you an ongoing sense of peace?

20___

20___

20___

Lord, let us be instruments of your peace.

APRIL 2

What's something you've never told anyone?

20__ _____

_____

_____

_____

20__ _____

_____

_____

_____

20__ _____

_____

_____

_____

You know us better than anyone, Lord—better than we know
ourselves—and you still love us. Thank you for that.

Flying? Invisibility? X-ray vision? What's
a superpower you wish you had?

20___

20___

20___

APRIL 9

Think of someone who stays calm even in stormy
seas. What can you learn from that person?

20___

20___

20___

*Lord, thank you for the fruits of the Spirit that we
see in others. Let us celebrate them.*

APRIL 5

Who's the peacemaker in your family?
How can you spread peace?

20___

20___

20___

"Make every effort to keep the unity of the Spirit
through the bond of peace." —EPHESIANS 4:3

What do you see as the biggest difference
between the two of you?

20___ _____

_____

_____

_____

20___ _____

_____

_____

_____

20___ _____

_____

_____

_____

_____

Lord, help us bridge the gap between us with mutual respect and love.

What's a valuable piece of advice you recently received?

20___

20___

20___

Give us a spirit of humility, Lord, and help us learn from others.

What advice would you give to your 12-year-old self?

20___

20___

20___

"The beginning of wisdom is this: Get wisdom. Though it
cost all you have, get understanding." —PROVERBS 4:7

What are some personality traits the two of you share?

20___

20___

20___

Heavenly Father, thank you for our similarities—and our differences.

What's one way that teenagers today seem
different from when you were teens?

20___ ___

20___ ___

20___ ___

What's something you're surprised to find yourself doing?

20____

20____

20____

Times seem to change quickly, Lord. Help us adapt and adjust.

What can you do today to deepen your relationships
with your kids or your friends' kids?

20____ _____

_____

_____

_____

20____ _____

_____

_____

_____

20____ _____

_____

_____

_____

"Fathers, do not exasperate your children; instead, bring them up
in the training and instruction of the Lord." —EPHESIANS 6:4

What's something you would be surprised and
delighted to hear your significant other suggest?

20___ _____

_____

_____

_____

20___ _____

_____

_____

_____

20___ _____

_____

_____

_____

_____

What are you currently putting off doing?

20___ _____

_____

_____

_____

20___ _____

_____

_____

_____

20___ _____

_____

_____

_____

_____

Let your priorities be our priorities, Lord.

What's something your taxes go to that you appreciate?

20___

_____

_____

_____

_____

20___

_____

_____

_____

_____

20___

_____

_____

_____

_____

"All the believers were together and had everything
in common. They sold property and possessions to
give to anyone who had need." —ACTS 2:44-45

APRIL 16

If time and money were no object, what
hobby would you like to pursue?

20___ _____

_____

_____

_____

20___ _____

_____

_____

_____

20___ _____

_____

_____

_____

*Heavenly Father, help us turn off the pressures
of the day and find rest and relaxation.*

If time and money were no object, where
would you like to serve as a volunteer?

20___

20___

20___

Lord, make us sensitive to the needs of people around us.

What's your favorite thing about the town you call home?

20___

20___

20___

What would you like to change about your town?

20___

_____

20___

_____

20___

_____

Dear God, give us courage to change what we should.

Who are you currently learning from? Is
there someone you can mentor?

20___
_____
_____
_____
_____

20___
_____
_____
_____
_____

20___
_____
_____
_____
_____
_____

*Lord, help us extend ourselves and share our
experience in gentle, affirming ways.*

APRIL 21

What got on your nerves today? What made you happy?

20___

20___

20___

"As God's chosen people, holy and dearly loved, clothe yourselves with compassion, kindness, humility, gentleness and patience." —COLOSSIANS 3:12

APRIL 22

I am the _____ one, according to my closest friends.

20___ _____

20___ _____

20___ _____

"I praise you because I am fearfully and wonderfully made; your works are wonderful, I know that full well." —PSALM 139:14

APRIL 23

Which of your friends most resembles
you? Who resembles you the least?

20___

20___

20___

Whom do you wish you lived closer to?

20___

20___

20___

Lord, strengthen our connections to loved ones far and near.

What's a helpful bit of constructive
criticism you recently received?

20___ _____

_____

_____

_____

20___ _____

_____

_____

_____

20___ _____

_____

_____

_____

_____

Help us not be too proud to be corrected now and then.

You're making a time capsule. What do you want
to be sure to include from this past year?

20___ _____

_____

_____

_____

20___ _____

_____

_____

_____

20___ _____

_____

_____

_____

_____

Not every day is memorable, Lord, but thank you for all of them.

APRIL 27

What's something you're not going to
miss about this past year?

20___

20___

20___

Choose one item from your wardrobe that you can
get rid of. What is it, and why would you pick it?

20___

_____

_____

_____

_____

20___

_____

_____

_____

_____

20___

_____

_____

_____

_____

Lord, help us not to be vain, but to value what you value.

APRIL 29

What's something that humbled you a little recently?

20___ _____

_____

_____

20___ _____

_____

_____

20___ _____

_____

_____

_____

"Pride goes before destruction, a haughty
spirit before a fall." —PROVERBS 16:18

You're getting the entire month of May off!
What do you want to do with that time?

20___

_____

_____

_____

_____

20___

_____

_____

_____

_____

20___

_____

_____

_____

_____

Options and choices surround us, Lord. Give us a
spirit of discernment regarding our time.

MAY 1

"The fruit of the Spirit is...forbearance" (Galatians 5:22).
Who or what is currently helping you practice patience?

20___ _____

_____

_____

_____

_____

20___ _____

_____

_____

_____

_____

20___ _____

_____

_____

_____

_____

As we face the trials that develop patience, Lord, we ask for calm spirits.

What's something nice you want to
say to each other right now?

20___ _____

_____

_____

_____

20___ _____

_____

_____

_____

20___ _____

_____

_____

_____

Give us gracious speech, Lord, especially for the ones we love.

What do you believe a good parent must do consistently well?

20__

20__

20__

"While he was still a long way off, his father saw him and was filled with compassion for him; he ran to his son, threw his arms around him and kissed him." —LUKE 15:20

What's been your favorite science fiction
or fantasy movie so far this year?

20___ _____

_____

_____

_____

_____

20___ _____

_____

_____

_____

_____

20___ _____

_____

_____

_____

_____

What did you enjoy about planning your wedding? If you're not yet married, what would you include in your dream wedding?

20___

20___

20___

What's your favorite part of your job?

20___

20___

20___

Thank you for work, Lord. Help us use our jobs to bring honor to you.

What's frustrating about your job? What can you change?

20___ _____

_____

_____

_____

_____

20___ _____

_____

_____

_____

20___ _____

_____

_____

_____

_____

We want to see struggles as opportunities for
growth. Please give us eyes to see.

Write about a time you needed to forgive someone.

20___ _____

_____

_____

_____

20___ _____

_____

_____

_____

20___ _____

_____

_____

_____

"If you do not forgive others their sins, your Father
will not forgive your sins." —MATTHEW 6:15

MAY 9

What's the most beautiful thing you've seen in the past year?

20___

20___

20___

Lord, thank you for the beauty that surrounds us.

What do you truly respect about each other?

20___ _____
_____
_____
_____
_____

20___ _____
_____
_____
_____
_____

20___ _____
_____
_____
_____
_____

*As our relationship has grown and continues
to grow, we give you thanks, Lord.*

What has surprised you most about being in a relationship?

20___

20___

20___

*We never stop being surprised and delighted
by our blessings. Thank you, Lord!*

MAY 12

When you look in the mirror, what's
something you're happy to see?

20___ _____

_____

_____

_____

20___ _____

_____

_____

_____

20___ _____

_____

_____

_____

"Now we see only a reflection as in a mirror; then we shall
see face to face. Now I know in part; then I shall know
fully, even as I am fully known." —1 CORINTHIANS 13:12

What's something that's recently become
popular, but you just don't get it at all?

20___

20___

20___

As the world around us changes, help us judge wisely.

What's something that's recently become
popular that you'd kind of like to try?

20___ _____

_____

_____

_____

20___ _____

_____

_____

_____

20___ _____

_____

_____

_____

_____

Lord, we thank you for the joys of adventure, spontaneity, and discovery.

Do you think kids should be rewarded for good
behavior, or is good behavior just expected?

20___ _____

_____

_____

_____

_____

20___ _____

_____

_____

_____

_____

20___ _____

_____

_____

_____

_____

"Start children off on the way they should go, and even when
they are old they will not turn from it." —PROVERBS 22:6

Would you rather be able to create a painting,
write a symphony, or direct a movie?

20__ __

20__ __

20__ __

Thank you for the gift of creativity, Lord.

What's something you see older generations
doing that you wish you were doing?

20___

_____

_____

_____

_____

20___

_____

_____

_____

_____

20___

_____

_____

_____

_____

_____

As we navigate this life, Lord, we ask for optimism and hope.

What's something you see older generations
doing that you hope you never do?

20___ _____

_____

_____

_____

20___ _____

_____

_____

_____

20___ _____

_____

_____

_____

Protect us from stubbornness and bitterness, Lord.

MAY 19

You can travel anywhere in the world to see a
live concert. Whom do you want to see?

20___

20___

20___

You can travel anywhere *in time* to see a live concert. Whom do you want to see?

20___
_____
_____
_____
_____

20___
_____
_____
_____
_____

20___
_____
_____
_____
_____

Whom would you like to get to know better in the next year?

20___

20___

20___

Give us energy to invest in the people around us, Lord.

What's something you feel less motivated
to do now than you did a year ago?

20___

20___

20___

Share a favorite pet (or other animal) memory.

20___

20___

20___

Lord, we thank you for our four-legged friends.

How are you making a difference in the
part of the world you influence?

20___

_____

_____

_____

_____

20___

_____

_____

_____

_____

20___

_____

_____

_____

_____

_____

*Help us take our roles in our community seriously,
Lord. Help us be a source of grace and peace.*

MAY 25

In what ways can you pray for each other today?

20___

20___

20___

"If you believe, you will receive whatever you
ask for in prayer." —MATTHEW 21:22

What's something you just can't get enough of?

20___ _____

_____

_____

_____

20___ _____

_____

_____

_____

20___ _____

_____

_____

_____

_____

Thank you for our many blessings, Lord.

Is there something you've always meant
to do but still haven't done?

20___ _____

_____

_____

_____

20___ _____

_____

_____

_____

20___ _____

_____

_____

_____

_____

Lord, help us keep learning and growing.

MAY 28

What's your ideal anniversary date?

20___

20___

20___

Lord, help us to always value each other.

What recent accomplishment made you
grateful for God's work in your life?

20___

20___

20___

"Humility is the fear of the LORD; its wages are riches
and honor and life." —PROVERBS 22:4

What do your friends admire about you?

20___ _____

_____

_____

_____

20___ _____

_____

_____

_____

20___ _____

_____

_____

_____

"I always thank my God for you because of his grace
given you in Christ Jesus." —1 CORINTHIANS 1:4

What do you think is a common misperception about you?

20__

20__

20__

"The fruit of the Spirit is...kindness" (Galatians 5:22).
What's a recent act of kindness you witnessed?

20___ _____

_____

_____

_____

20___ _____

_____

_____

_____

20___ _____

_____

_____

_____

_____

"The LORD appeared to us in the past, saying: 'I have
loved you with an everlasting love; I have drawn you
with unfailing kindness.'" —JEREMIAH 31:3

What kind of family vacation would you most like to take?

20___

20___

20___

Thank you, God, for the times we enjoy with our families.

What's something your parents could have done better?

20___

20___

20___

*Lord, forgive our parents for their shortcomings
as we seek to be forgiven for our own.*

JUNE 9

If you were to write (or rewrite) your wedding
vows, what would you want them to say?

20___

_____

_____

_____

_____

20___

_____

_____

_____

_____

20___

_____

_____

_____

_____

"On the third day a wedding took place at Cana in
Galilee. Jesus' mother was there, and Jesus and his disciples
had also been invited to the wedding." —JOHN 2:1-2

If you could have a destination wedding (or marriage getaway)
wherever you wanted, where in the world would you go?

20___

20___

20___

Lord, we praise you for this big, wonderful world.

JUNE 6

It's summer blockbuster time! What's been
your favorite movie so far this year?

20___

20___

20___

When our culture tells us who or what is important,
Lord, help us keep our eyes on you.

What's your favorite food to eat outdoors?

20___ _____
_____
_____
_____

20___ _____
_____
_____
_____

20___ _____
_____
_____
_____

"Everything that lives and moves about will be food for you. Just as I gave you the green plants, I now give you everything." —GENESIS 9:3

JUNE 8

Were you usually glad to see the school year
end? What did you like about school?

20___

20___

20___

What experiences would you like to
share with the next generation?

20___ _____

_____

_____

_____

_____

20___ _____

_____

_____

_____

_____

20___ _____

_____

_____

_____

_____

As we see ourselves in those younger than us, Lord,
may we be blessed by what we find.

What's something you're currently doing
that you have some doubts about?

20___

20___

20___

"When you ask [God for wisdom], you must believe and
not doubt, because the one who doubts is like a wave of
the sea, blown and tossed by the wind." —JAMES 1:6

What were your parents' expectations for you? How do you feel you're doing at living them out?

20___ _____

_____

_____

_____

_____

20___ _____

_____

_____

_____

_____

20___ _____

_____

_____

_____

_____

Sometimes the hardest thing to see is our true self. Give us insight, Lord.

What's one act of kindness you could do in the next few days?

20___

20___

20___

Lord, make us aware of the needs around us.

JUNE 13

When was the last time you felt truly embarrassed?

20___

_____

20___

_____

20___

_____

Thank you for unexpected opportunities to learn humility, Lord.

JUNE 14

Has anything recently made you feel as
though you're doing pretty well?

20___

20___

20___

"Blessed is the one who trusts in the LORD, whose
confidence is in him." —JEREMIAH 17:7

Give each other an original compliment.

20___ _____

_____

_____

_____

20___ _____

_____

_____

_____

20___ _____

_____

_____

_____

_____

Father God, help us be generous with our words.

What's something you agreed to and then second-guessed?

20___

20___

20___

Give us the wisdom to know we're not always
right, and help us be gracious about that.

You can return one item with no penalty and have your money cheerfully refunded. What is it?

20___ _____

_____

_____

_____

_____

20___ _____

_____

_____

_____

_____

20___ _____

_____

_____

_____

_____

"Watch out! Be on your guard against all kinds of greed; life does not consist in an abundance of possessions." —LUKE 12:15

What's something you learned when you were
young that seems even truer now?

20_ _

20_ _

20_ _

Growing older gracefully is an art, Lord. Help us find ways to practice it.

If you could solve one issue that plagues the
entire world, what would you solve?

20___ _____

_____

_____

_____

_____

20___ _____

_____

_____

_____

20___ _____

_____

_____

_____

_____

Thank you for the little differences we can make in the world around us.

JUNE 20

Does time seem as if it's going faster,
slower, or about the same?

20___ _____

_____

_____

_____

20___ _____

_____

_____

_____

20___ _____

_____

_____

_____

_____

"Do not forget this one thing, dear friends: With the Lord a day is like
a thousand years, and a thousand years are like a day." —2 PETER 3:8

What's something that shouts *summer* to you?

20___

_____

_____

_____

_____

20___

_____

_____

_____

_____

20___

_____

_____

_____

_____

We can so easily get caught up in what seems important,
Lord. Help us find time to relax and recharge.

Recall a memory from a favorite vacation.

20___

_____

_____

_____

_____

20___

_____

_____

_____

_____

20___

_____

_____

_____

_____

We give our praise to the One who holds the
past, the present, and the future.

What's something that never fails to energize you?

20___ _____

_____

_____

_____

20___ _____

_____

_____

_____

20___ _____

_____

_____

_____

_____

"He gives strength to the weary and increases
the power of the weak." —ISAIAH 40:29

What's something that never fails to drain you?

20___

_____

_____

_____

_____

20___

_____

_____

_____

_____

20___

_____

_____

_____

_____

We can get grumbly when we're tired, Lord. Give us patience and grace.

What's something you feel you're getting
better and better at over time?

20___ _____

_____

_____

_____

20___ _____

_____

_____

_____

20___ _____

_____

_____

_____

_____

Thank you for the gifts you've given each of us, Lord.

JUNE 26

Whose life is a little better because of
something you've done lately?

20___

20___

20___

"Truly I tell you, whatever you did for one of the least of these
brothers and sisters of mine, you did for me." —MATTHEW 25:40

When do you feel the most vulnerable?

20__ _____
_____
_____
_____
_____

20__ _____
_____
_____
_____
_____

20__ _____
_____
_____
_____
_____

Help us find our strength and security in you, Lord.

What's a trait you have that you hope to see in
your kids (or in anyone you influence)?

20___ _____

_____

_____

_____

_____

20___ _____

_____

_____

_____

_____

20___ _____

_____

_____

_____

_____

Help us remember that people are watching and learning from us, Lord.

What's a trait you have that you hope you won't
see in your kids (or in anyone you influence)?

20___ _____

_____

_____

_____

20___ _____

_____

_____

_____

20___ _____

_____

_____

_____

_____

*Lord, forgive us when we don't live up to the
standards you hold for us, and help us repent.*

What's something you can do as a couple to
increase kindness right where you are?

20___ _____

_____

_____

_____

20___ _____

_____

_____

_____

20___ _____

_____

_____

_____

"He has shown you, O mortal, what is good. And what does
the LORD require of you? To act justly and to love mercy
and to walk humbly with your God." —MICAH 6:8

"The fruit of the Spirit is...goodness" (Galatians 5:22). How can you demonstrate goodness in a new way this month?

20_ _ _____

_____

_____

_____

20_ _ _____

_____

_____

_____

20_ _ _____

_____

_____

_____

Thank you for the goodness that surrounds us, Lord.

JULY 2

What's something you always look forward to doing together?

20___

20___

20___

Lord, we give you the credit as our relationship
continues to grow and deepen.

You've just received exciting news! Which
three people do you call first?

20___ _____

_____

_____

_____

20___ _____

_____

_____

_____

20___ _____

_____

_____

_____

"When Elizabeth heard Mary's greeting, the baby leaped in her
womb, and Elizabeth was filled with the Holy Spirit." —LUKE 1:41

JULY 4

Are you more or less patriotic than you used to be?

20___ ___

20___ ___

20___ ___

We enjoy so many freedoms and privileges,
Lord. Thank you for those blessings.

Do you prefer to sit in the front row or the back row at church?

20___

20___

20___

"Not giving up meeting together, as some are in the habit
of doing, but encouraging one another—and all the more
as you see the Day approaching." —HEBREWS 10:25

You can be someone else for one day. Whom do you choose?

20___

20___

20___

Thank you for our distinct and individual personalities, Lord.

You switch places with each other for one
day. What's the first thing you do?

20___ _____

_____

_____

_____

20___ _____

_____

_____

_____

20___ _____

_____

_____

_____

_____

*When we know each other well, we're tempted to take
each other for granted. Help us be grateful.*

What's something you find yourself doing
that your parents used to do?

20___

20___

20___

*Influence can be good—and it can be less than
good. Help us focus on the best.*

What's a gift you can give each other today?

20___ _____

_____

_____

_____

20___ _____

_____

_____

_____

20___ _____

_____

_____

_____

"It is by grace you have been saved, through faith—and this is
not from yourselves, it is the gift of God." —EPHESIANS 2:8

How do you express your creativity?

20___

20___

20___

Let us celebrate the variety and diversity of the
gifts you've given our faith community.

Who's been an influence on you in the past week?

20___ _____

_____

_____

_____

20___ _____

_____

_____

_____

20___ _____

_____

_____

_____

Thank you for the people who continue to inform our lives, Lord.

Who's a spiritual leader you admire or are inspired by?

20___

20___

20___

"Remember your leaders, who spoke the word of God to you. Consider
the outcome of their way of life and imitate their faith." —HEBREWS 13:7

What's something you've recently come
to appreciate about each other?

20___ _____

_____

_____

_____

_____

20___ _____

_____

_____

_____

20___ _____

_____

_____

_____

_____

Thank you for your plan for our lives, Lord, and
the fun surprises along the way.

What's your dream job or dream retirement plan?

20___

20___

20___

At our jobs and in our leisure time, Lord, help us glorify you.

What product or service is worth paying top dollar?

20___

_____

_____

_____

_____

20___

_____

_____

_____

_____

20___

_____

_____

_____

_____

_____

Teach us the true value of what we have and keep
us from coveting what we don't have.

Write about a tough situation that ended
up teaching you a valuable lesson.

20___ _____

_____

_____

_____

20___ _____

_____

_____

_____

20___ _____

_____

_____

_____

"We know that in all things God works for the good of those who love
him, who have been called according to his purpose." —ROMANS 8:28

Which of your five senses do you value most?

20___ _____

_____

_____

_____

20___ _____

_____

_____

_____

20___ _____

_____

_____

_____

_____

*Lord, thank you for so many wonderful things
to see, hear, touch, taste, and smell.*

Which musical instrument do you wish you could play?

20___

20___

20___

Creator God, thank you for the music you've put in our hearts.

What's something your parents did well?

20_ _

20_ _

20_ _

"Children's children are a crown to the aged, and parents
are the pride of their children." —PROVERBS 17:6

JULY 20

What's something you're currently
doing that you feel good about?

20___

20___

20___

Lord, thank you for small successes.

JULY 21

What would you like to have written on your tombstone?

20___

20___

20___

Help us remember that we're always building our legacies.

What's a phrase you use too much?

20___

20___

20___

"Let your conversation be always full of grace, seasoned with salt, so that you may know how to answer everyone." —COLOSSIANS 4:6

JULY 23

What do you think is going to be the
hardest part of the week ahead?

20___

_____

_____

_____

_____

20___

_____

_____

_____

_____

20___

_____

_____

_____

_____

Challenges and struggles are going to come. Keep us steadfast, Lord.

What do you think is going to be the
best part of the week ahead?

20___

20___

20___

Joys and celebrations are going to come. Keep us grateful, Lord.

Are you more likely to skydive, windsurf,
or ski down a mountainside?

20___

20___

20___

Keep us safe and wise but ready for the occasional adventure.

Do you think you're easy to read? How can you be more open?

20___ _____

_____

_____

_____

20___ _____

_____

_____

_____

20___ _____

_____

_____

_____

_____

"Whoever walks in integrity walks securely, but whoever
takes crooked paths will be found out." —PROVERBS 10:9

In what area of your life could you be more decisive?

20___ _____

_____

_____

_____

20___ _____

_____

_____

_____

20___ _____

_____

_____

_____

Lord, guide us in saying yes or no to things others ask of us.

When have you felt balanced?

20___ _____

_____

_____

_____

_____

20___ _____

_____

_____

_____

_____

20___ _____

_____

_____

_____

_____

Thank you for the gift of a calm spirit.

When have you felt off-balance?

20___

20___

20___

When the storms rage, Lord, remind us where to find peace.

JULY 30

Everyone has a hidden talent. What's one of yours?

20__

20__

20__

"We have different gifts, according to the grace
given to each of us." —ROMANS 12:6

What's something you feel people get wrong about you?

20___

_____

20___

_____

20___

_____

Help us not worry so much about how people see us and instead try to understand others.

"The fruit of the Spirit is...faithfulness" (Galatians 5:22).
Who demonstrates faithfulness in your life?

20___

20___

20___

"Because of the LORD's great love we are not consumed, for
his compassions never fail. They are new every morning;
great is your faithfulness." —LAMENTATIONS 3:22-23

What's something one of you said in the past
week that made the other feel loved?

20___

_____

_____

_____

_____

20___

_____

_____

_____

_____

20___

_____

_____

_____

_____

_____

Guide us toward joy, faithfulness, and love.

What's a surefire way to rekindle your
connection to each other?

20_ _

20_ _

20_ _

Help us see the best in each other, Lord.

How have you passed on your faith to those younger than you?

20___ _____

_____

_____

_____

20___ _____

_____

_____

_____

20___ _____

_____

_____

_____

_____

"Jesus called the children to him and said, 'Let the little children come to me, and do not hinder them, for the kingdom of God belongs to such as these.'" —LUKE 18:16

AUGUST 5

What gets in the way of good communication?
How can you overcome those obstacles?

20___

20___

20___

Help us recognize roadblocks, Lord, and direct us to your truth.

What's a topic you should always discuss in person?

20___

20___

20___

*Thank you for the quiet moments we find with
you, Lord, and with each other.*

What's something you would like others
to understand more about you?

20___

20___

20___

"Is not wisdom found among the aged? Does not
long life bring understanding?" —JOB 12:12

What's something from your past that
profoundly impacts you today?

20___

20___

20___

Help us learn from the past without being burdened by it.

Insensitive? Overly sensitive? Just right?
Where do you see yourself?

20___

20___

20___

Lord, give us grace with everyone—and a double portion with each other.

You're going swimming. Salt water, fresh water, or chlorinated water?

20___

20___

20___

"God created the great creatures of the sea and every living thing with which the water teems and that moves about in it, according to their kinds." —GENESIS 1:21

AUGUST 11

How can you can show support to each other today?

20___

_____

_____

_____

_____

20___

_____

_____

_____

_____

20___

_____

_____

_____

_____

Help us show greater love to each other.

What's something you're hesitant to share?

20___ _____

_____

_____

_____

20___ _____

_____

_____

_____

20___ _____

_____

_____

_____

_____

Help us tear down the walls we build between us, Lord.

AUGUST 13

What's something you have no intention of
compromising on, no matter what?

20___

20___

20___

Show us where we're being stubborn, even if it hurts.

How is the nature of physical affection changing
for you? How much seems right?

20___

20___

20___

"He who finds a wife finds what is good and receives
favor from the LORD." —PROVERBS 18:22

Is it possible to share too much? Do you know someone who does this?

20___ _____

_____

_____

_____

20___ _____

_____

_____

_____

20___ _____

_____

_____

_____

_____

"I am afraid that when I come I may not find you as I want
you to be, and you may not find me as you want me to be. I
fear that there may be discord, jealousy, fits of rage, selfish
ambition, slander, gossip, arrogance and disorder." —2 CORINTHIANS 12:20

AUGUST 16

What's a summer activity you've never
tried but might like to do?

20___ _____
_____
_____
_____
_____

20___ _____
_____
_____
_____
_____

20___ _____
_____
_____
_____
_____

Keep showing us how to have fun, Lord.

When do you feel most in sync as a couple?

20___ _____

_____

_____

_____

20___ _____

_____

_____

_____

20___ _____

_____

_____

_____

Thank you for the comfort that comes from knowing each other well.

When do you feel most out of sync as a couple?

20___

20___

20___

It might feel like we ask this often, but give
us patience with each other, Lord.

How can you make a special summer memory for each other?

20___

20___

20___

"I thank my God every time I remember you." —PHILIPPIANS 1:3

What's something each of you could do
less of for the other's sake?

20___ _____

_____

_____

_____

20___ _____

_____

_____

_____

20___ _____

_____

_____

_____

_____

Show us where we're being proud, Lord, and make us willing to change.

What's the most positive thing you
can do as a couple right now?

20___ _____

_____

_____

_____

_____

20___ _____

_____

_____

_____

_____

20___ _____

_____

_____

_____

_____

We ask for wisdom, insight, and open hearts.

What are you doing as a couple that
you'd like others to emulate?

20___ _____

_____

_____

_____

_____

20___ _____

_____

_____

_____

_____

20___ _____

_____

_____

_____

_____

"Follow my example, as I follow the example
of Christ." —1 CORINTHIANS 11:1

What are you doing as a couple that others should try to avoid?

20___

_____

_____

_____

_____

20___

_____

_____

_____

_____

20___

_____

_____

_____

_____

We know we're not perfect, Lord. Show us where we can repent and grow.

How can you improve your methods of resolving conflict?

20___

20___

20___

Help us diminish tension and look for common ground.

What would your grandparents think of
how you spent the past year?

20__ _____

_____

_____

_____

_____

20__ _____

_____

_____

_____

_____

20__ _____

_____

_____

_____

_____

*Thank you for the example of our families, Lord, and
for the blessings they've passed on.*

Do you believe you both spend enough time
talking about your relationship?

20___ _____

_____

_____

_____

20___ _____

_____

_____

_____

20___ _____

_____

_____

_____

"There is a time for everything, and a season for every
activity under the heavens." —ECCLESIASTES 3:1

Who is the more introverted of the two of you?
How does that affect your relationship?

20___ _____

_____

_____

_____

_____

20___ _____

_____

_____

_____

_____

20___ _____

_____

_____

_____

_____

You've given each of us different personalities, Lord. Help us celebrate that.

Who is the more extroverted of the two of you?
How does that affect your relationship?

20___ _____

_____

_____

_____

_____

20___ _____

_____

_____

_____

_____

20___ _____

_____

_____

_____

_____

Show us how to be great resources for each other.

What's getting in the way of your "together
time"? What can you do about that?

20___

20___

20___

"I do not want to see you now and make only a passing visit; I hope to
spend some time with you, if the Lord permits." —1 CORINTHIANS 16:7

Among your current friends, whom do
you wish you saw more often?

20___ _____

_____

_____

_____

20___ _____

_____

_____

_____

20___ _____

_____

_____

_____

_____

Thank you for the people you've put in our lives.

Among your current friends, who do you
think could be shown more love?

20___

20___

20___

*Show us what we can learn from everyone we
know, even people we find challenging.*

"The fruit of the Spirit is...gentleness" (Galatians 5:22-23).
Who is a good example of gentleness to you?

20___ _____

_____

_____

_____

20___ _____

_____

_____

_____

20___ _____

_____

_____

_____

"A bruised reed he will not break, and a smoldering
wick he will not snuff out." —ISAIAH 42:3

Who was one of your favorite teachers when you
were in school? Who's teaching you now?

20___

_____

_____

_____

_____

_____

20___

_____

_____

_____

_____

20___

_____

_____

_____

_____

Lord, we ask for a lifetime of teachers and a teachable spirit.

What recent purchase was totally worth it?

20___ _____

_____

_____

_____

20___ _____

_____

_____

_____

20___ _____

_____

_____

_____

_____

Show us how to own things without them owning us.

SEPTEMBER 9

What recent purchase was totally *not* worth it?

20___ _____

_____

_____

_____

20___ _____

_____

_____

_____

20___ _____

_____

_____

_____

"Do not store up for yourselves treasures on earth, where moths and vermin destroy, and where thieves break in and steal." —MATTHEW 6:19

Would you rather visit someone's house
or have someone visit yours?

20___

_____

_____

_____

_____

20___

_____

_____

_____

_____

20___

_____

_____

_____

_____

Help us share the gift of hospitality, Lord.

What's the perfect amount of time to
spend with extended family?

20_ _

20_ _

20_ _

Thank you for our aunts, uncles, and cousins.
Help us be gracious to all of them.

SEPTEMBER 7

What's something you have a hard time
responding to in a gentle way?

20___

20___

20___

"A gentle answer turns away wrath, but a harsh
word stirs up anger." —PROVERBS 15:1

Which three values do you treasure above all the rest?

20___

_____

_____

_____

_____

20___

_____

_____

_____

_____

20___

_____

_____

_____

_____

Show us how to make the most of our gifts
and appreciate the gifts of others.

What can you do to live out your values more consistently?

20__

_____

_____

_____

_____

20__

_____

_____

_____

_____

20__

_____

_____

_____

_____

_____

Lord, give us honest assessments of ourselves.

SEPTEMBER 10

How can you be intentional about passing
on values to the next generation?

20___

20___

20___

What's something you could begin doing this
fall to improve your physical well-being?

20___ _____

_____

_____

_____

_____

20___ _____

_____

_____

_____

_____

20___ _____

_____

_____

_____

_____

Help us get outside and enjoy your creation, Lord.

What's going on at work right now that you feel good about?

20___

20___

20___

Thank you for accomplishments large and small.

How can your attitude toward work improve this year?

20___ _____

_____

_____

_____

20___ _____

_____

_____

_____

20___ _____

_____

_____

_____

_____

"Go to the ant, you sluggard; consider its
ways and be wise!" —PROVERBS 6:6

SEPTEMBER 19

Which parenting skill do you believe
you are (or could be) best at?

20___

20___

20___

What can you talk about with your kids (or a relative's kids) now that used to be off-limits?

20___ _____

_____

_____

_____

20___ _____

_____

_____

_____

20___ _____

_____

_____

_____

_____

Show us how to be good guides through all the stages of growth.

SEPTEMBER 16

What's something about today's high
schoolers that mystifies you?

20___ _____

_____

_____

_____

_____

20___ _____

_____

_____

_____

20___ _____

_____

_____

_____

Lord, don't let us be easily agitated.

How have your spending habits changed this year?

20___

_____

_____

_____

_____

20___

_____

_____

_____

_____

20___

_____

_____

_____

_____

_____

"The love of money is a root of all kinds of evil. Some people, eager for money, have wandered from the faith and pierced themselves with many griefs." —1 TIMOTHY 6:10

How can you be there for each other this week?

20___ _____

_____

_____

_____

20___ _____

_____

_____

_____

20___ _____

_____

_____

_____

_____

Show us how to meet each other's needs, Lord.

Do you have a plan for what will happen in the event of your death? Is this something you can easily discuss?

20___

20___

20___

Give us the ability to talk about difficult topics with grace.

SEPTEMBER 20

What would you like to be remembered for?

20___

20___

20___

"A good name is more desirable than great riches; to be
esteemed is better than silver or gold." —PROVERBS 22:1

What are some activities you used to do that you miss doing?

20___ _____

_____

_____

_____

20___ _____

_____

_____

_____

20___ _____

_____

_____

_____

_____

Lord, help us be realistic about what we can and can't do.

What's one of your favorite TV shows from the past?

20___

20___

20___

*Show us how to enjoy nostalgia while living in
the present and hoping for the future.*

What's your current comfort food and why?

20___ _____

_____

_____

_____

20___ _____

_____

_____

_____

20___ _____

_____

_____

_____

"Bring the fattened calf and kill it. Let's have
a feast and celebrate." —LUKE 15:23

How can you balance being gentle with being strong?

20___ _____

_____

_____

_____

20___ _____

_____

_____

_____

20___ _____

_____

_____

_____

Teach us to be gentle, Lord.

Can you think of someone you need to forgive?

20___

_____

_____

_____

_____

20___

_____

_____

_____

_____

20___

_____

_____

_____

_____

"Forgive us our debts, as we also have forgiven
our debtors." —MATTHEW 6:12

Is there something for which you need to forgive yourself?

20___

_____

_____

_____

_____

20___

_____

_____

_____

_____

20___

_____

_____

_____

_____

Remind us when we need to be gentle with ourselves as well as with others.

What's something you heard at church
recently that made you think?

20___

20___

20___

*We can take our faith communities for granted,
Lord. Help us see you in them instead.*

SEPTEMBER 28

What are some ways you can sincerely compliment each other?

20___

20___

20___

We're so grateful for each other, Lord. Thank you!

Would you say you're more or less
competitive than you used to be?

20__ _____

_____

_____

_____

20__ _____

_____

_____

_____

20__ _____

_____

_____

_____

"Do you not know that in a race all the runners run, but only one gets
the prize? Run in such a way as to get the prize." —1 CORINTHIANS 9:24

If you're going to eat a big meal, what is your food of choice?

20___

20___

20___

"The fruit of the Spirit is...self-control" (Galatians 5:22-23).
Has your self-control improved this year? Why or why not?

20____ _____

_____

_____

_____

_____

20____ _____

_____

_____

_____

_____

20____ _____

_____

_____

_____

_____

*Dear God, show us where we lack self-control
and help us nurture and develop it.*

I know I should _____ more.

20__ _____

_____

_____

_____

20__ _____

_____

_____

_____

20__ _____

_____

_____

_____

"Everyone who competes in the games goes into strict training.
They do it to get a crown that will not last, but we do it to
get a crown that will last forever." —1 CORINTHIANS 9:25

I know I should _____ less.

20___ _____
_____
_____
_____

20___ _____
_____
_____
_____

20___ _____
_____
_____
_____

Lord, teach us restraint.

Which three traits do you truly admire in each other?

20___

20___

20___

Help us remember to build each other up.

OCTOBER 5

Which three traits do you most like about yourself?

20___ _____

_____

_____

_____

20___ _____

_____

_____

_____

20___ _____

_____

_____

_____

_____

Grant us a clear, honest, and humble view of ourselves.

OCTOBER 6

What do you like best about autumn?

20___

_____

_____

_____

_____

20___

_____

_____

_____

_____

20___

_____

_____

_____

_____

"Let the fields be jubilant, and everything in them; let all
the trees of the forest sing for joy." —PSALM 96:12

What part of being in a relationship is a
challenge to your self-control?

20___ _____

_____

_____

_____

20___ _____

_____

_____

_____

20___ _____

_____

_____

_____

Show us how to love better and better, Lord.

What is something positive you can
say to each other every day?

20___

20___

20___

Lord, may our words to each other be rooted in our love for you.

When was the last time you felt absolutely free?

20__ _____

_____

_____

_____

20__ _____

_____

_____

_____

20__ _____

_____

_____

_____

_____

"The Lord is the Spirit, and where the Spirit of the Lord
is, there is freedom." —2 CORINTHIANS 3:17

What's a healthy habit you can practice?

20___ _____

20___ _____

20___ _____

Help us think of our bodies as vessels for your Spirit.

When was the last time your instincts were rewarded?

20___

_____

_____

_____

_____

20___

_____

_____

_____

_____

20___

_____

_____

_____

_____

"Better a patient person than a warrior, one with self-control than one who takes a city." —PROVERBS 16:32

OCTOBER 12

When has skepticism kept you from doing
something that might have been good?

20___

_____

_____

_____

_____

20___

_____

_____

_____

_____

20___

_____

_____

_____

_____

_____

Give me courage to obey you in whatever you might ask of me.

In general, are you more or less open than you'd like
to be? How can you help each other in this area?

20___

20___

20___

Help us give up our defenses with each other.

If you could enlist your significant other's support in a self-improvement project, what would that project be?

20___

20___

20___

Show us how to hold each other accountable in a loving way.

Does thinking about school inspire happy
or less-than-happy memories?

20___

_____

_____

_____

_____

20___

_____

_____

_____

_____

20___

_____

_____

_____

_____

How can you improve the communication in your relationship?

20__ _____

_____

_____

_____

_____

20__ _____

_____

_____

_____

_____

20__ _____

_____

_____

_____

_____

"My dear brothers and sisters, take note of this: Everyone should be quick to listen, slow to speak and slow to become angry." —JAMES 1:19

OCTOBER 17

You're sitting around a firepit with your closest friends. Who's there?

20___ _____

_____

_____

_____

20___ _____

_____

_____

_____

20___ _____

_____

_____

_____

"One who has unreliable friends soon comes to ruin, but there is a friend who sticks closer than a brother." —PROVERBS 18:24

Are you more or less generous than you
used to be—or would like to be?

20___

20___

20___

Lord, help us hold our possessions loosely, remembering
that all good gifts come from you.

Many people have trouble controlling their
spending. How do you think you're doing?

20___ _____

_____

_____

_____

20___ _____

_____

_____

_____

20___ _____

_____

_____

_____

*We're surrounded by so many things. Father, give
us insight into what really matters.*

OCTOBER 20

What's a headline from this week's news that concerns you?

20___
_____
_____
_____
_____

20___
_____
_____
_____
_____

20___
_____
_____
_____
_____

"Peace I leave with you; my peace I give you. I do not
give to you as the world gives. Do not let your hearts
be troubled and do not be afraid." —JOHN 14:27

OCTOBER 21

What's a headline from this week's news
that makes you optimistic?

20___ _____

_____

_____

_____

20___ _____

_____

_____

_____

20___ _____

_____

_____

_____

Thank you for our eternal hope.

Do you need to apologize to someone?

20___

_____

20___

_____

20___

_____

Help us not let our pride stand in the way of
being the people you want us to be.

OCTOBER 23

What's something you're putting off that just needs to be done?

20__ __

20__ __

20__ __

"Whoever watches the wind will not plant; whoever looks
at the clouds will not reap." —ECCLESIASTES 11:4

Are you rushing through your day, or are you
taking time to smell the proverbial roses?

20__ __

20__ __

20__ __

Lord, help us stop to smell the proverbial roses—and the actual roses too.

If you want to enjoy a fancy meal, where do you go?

20___

20___

20___

Thank you, God, for simple pleasures.

Who's been challenging your thinking lately?

20__

20__

20__

"Show me your ways, LORD, teach me your paths." —PSALM 25:4

If you were to go slightly out of your
comfort zone, what would you try?

20___

20___

20___

Keep us ever growing and challenging ourselves.

What's a little blessing that you could focus on
and intentionally express gratitude for?

20___

20___

20___

Give us an abundance of gratitude, Lord.

When was the last time you felt scared?

20___

20___

20___

"Have I not commanded you? Be strong and courageous.
Do not be afraid; do not be discouraged, for the LORD your
God will be with you wherever you go." —JOSHUA 1:9

What's a snack that really challenges your self-control?

20___

20___

20___

Lord, help us avoid temptations in whatever forms they appear.

What's the most interesting costume you've
ever worn or seen someone wear?

20___ ___ _____

_____

_____

_____

_____

20___ ___ _____

_____

_____

_____

_____

20___ ___ _____

_____

_____

_____

_____

NOVEMBER 1

November is a great time to think about gratitude. What are three things you truly appreciate right now?

20___

_____

_____

_____

_____

20___

_____

_____

_____

20___

_____

_____

_____

_____

"Give thanks to the LORD, for he is good; his love endures forever." —PSALM 107:1

NOVEMBER 2

What's something you're grateful for
when it comes to your job?

20___

20___

20___

Thank you, Lord, for honorable work and the blessings we receive from it.

What's something you're grateful for about your upbringing?

20__ _____

_____

_____

_____

20__ _____

_____

_____

_____

20__ _____

_____

_____

_____

We travel different paths, Lord, but you guide
them all. Thank you for watching over us.

What makes you grateful for your current church home?

20____

20____

20____

"Thanks be to God, who always leads us as captives in Christ's
triumphal procession and uses us to spread the aroma of the
knowledge of him everywhere." —2 CORINTHIANS 2:14

How has your family made you grateful?

20___
_____
_____
_____
_____

20___
_____
_____
_____
_____

20___
_____
_____
_____
_____

We continually thank you for our families.

What's one way your body makes you grateful?

20__ _____

_____

_____

_____

20__ _____

_____

_____

_____

20__ _____

_____

_____

_____

*Lord, thank you for every walk, every stretch, every
little way we can bring honor to you.*

NOVEMBER 7

What are three things about your significant other
that make you extra grateful right now?

20__ _____

_____

_____

_____

20__ _____

_____

_____

_____

20__ _____

_____

_____

_____

"Make sure that nobody pays back wrong for wrong, but
always strive to do what is good for each other and
for everyone else." —1 THESSALONIANS 5:15

Would you ever consider running for
political office? Why or why not?

20___

20___

20___

Bless our leaders, Lord, and please give them wisdom.

NOVEMBER 9

If you did run for office—and you won!—
what's a law you'd change?

20___

20___

20___

NOVEMBER 10

Winter is coming. Do you mind spending it at home, or is there somewhere else you'd rather ride out the next few months?

20___ _____

_____

_____

_____

20___ _____

_____

_____

_____

20___ _____

_____

_____

_____

"My people will live in peaceful dwelling places, in secure homes, in undisturbed places of rest." —ISAIAH 32:18

Look around your house. Which appliance
has made your life much better?

20__ _____
_____
_____
_____

20__ _____
_____
_____
_____

20__ _____
_____
_____
_____

*Heavenly Father, please remind us that even
little things are gifts from you.*

Which room in your house would you like to
change, and how would you change it?

20___ _____

_____

_____

_____

20___ _____

_____

_____

_____

20___ _____

_____

_____

_____

Protect us from an unhealthy desire to keep up with those around us.

If you were going to be just a little more open than usual
with each other, what would you begin talking about?

20___ _____

_____

_____

_____

20___ _____

_____

_____

_____

20___ _____

_____

_____

_____

"Whoever would love life and see good days must keep their tongue
from evil and their lips from deceitful speech." —1 PETER 3:10

What challenge do you need to discuss
and prepare to handle together?

20___ _____

_____

_____

_____

_____

20___ _____

_____

_____

_____

_____

20___ _____

_____

_____

_____

_____

Lord, show us how to be the best versions of ourselves.

Whom would you like to invite for Thanksgiving
dinner? Whom should you invite?

20___

20___

20___

What's a concrete way you can show each
other some appreciation this week?

20___ _____

_____

_____

_____

_____

20___ _____

_____

_____

_____

20___ _____

_____

_____

_____

_____

"Give thanks in all circumstances; for this is God's will
for you in Christ Jesus." —1 THESSALONIANS 5:18

NOVEMBER 17

What's a skill you feel you lack but appreciate in others?

20__ _____

20__ _____

20__ _____

Help us avoid jealousy wherever it might tempt us.

Of the people in your church, small group, or Sunday school class, whom could you thank for their efforts?

20___ _____

_____

_____

_____

_____

20___ _____

_____

_____

_____

20___ _____

_____

_____

_____

Don't let us underestimate the power of positive affirmation.

NOVEMBER 19

Whom are you grateful for at work, in your neighborhood, or elsewhere in your day-to-day life?

20___

20___

20___

"Devote yourselves to prayer, being watchful and thankful." —COLOSSIANS 4:2

What song sums up this year for you?

20___ _____

_____

_____

_____

_____

20___ _____

_____

_____

_____

_____

20___ _____

_____

_____

_____

_____

Whether we can sing or not, thank you for the gift of music.

NOVEMBER 21

Which do you enjoy wearing more—gloves or scarves?

20__

_____

_____

_____

_____

20__

_____

_____

_____

_____

20__

_____

_____

_____

_____

"The LORD God made garments of skin for Adam and
his wife and clothed them." —GENESIS 3:21

NOVEMBER 22

How do you feel about hayrides and other fall activities?

20_ _

20_ _

20_ _

Thank you for youth, Lord.

NOVEMBER 23

How much do you look forward to days off from work?

20___ _____

_____

_____

_____

20___ _____

_____

_____

_____

20___ _____

_____

_____

_____

*We look forward to work, and we look forward
to rest. Thank you, Lord, for both.*

Describe your perfect Thanksgiving. What can you
do to make this year closer to your vision?

20__ _____

_____

_____

_____

_____

20__ _____

_____

_____

_____

20__ _____

_____

_____

_____

_____

"From them will come songs of thanksgiving and
the sound of rejoicing." —JEREMIAH 30:19

What's something you like even more about
each other now than when you met?

20___

20___

20___

As we grow older, thank you for the deeper, richer relationships we enjoy.

You're heading for warmer climates. How long
would the two of you last in an RV together?

20___

20___

20___

NOVEMBER 27

Can you find a nugget of gratitude in one of
the biggest challenges of your year?

20__ _____

_____

_____

_____

_____

20__ _____

_____

_____

_____

_____

20__ _____

_____

_____

_____

_____

"I will give thanks to you, LORD, with all my heart; I will
tell of all your wonderful deeds." —PSALM 9:1

Christians are the light of the world (Matthew 5:14).
How can you shed some light this holiday season?

20___

20___

20___

Don't let us hide our light, Lord. Help us shine.

Do you have your holiday shopping
done, or have you put it off?

20__ __

_____
_____
_____
_____
_____

20__ __

_____
_____
_____
_____
_____

20__ __

_____
_____
_____
_____
_____

Heavenly Father, keep us from procrastinating.

Whom do you want to affirm and support in the days
to come? (Think of some ways to do just that.)

20___

20___

20___

"Ever since I heard about your faith in the Lord Jesus and your
love for all God's people, I have not stopped giving thanks for
you, remembering you in my prayers." —EPHESIANS 1:15-16

What holiday traditions do you wish your family had
celebrated? How might you incorporate them now?

20__

_____

_____

_____

_____

20__

_____

_____

_____

_____

20__

_____

_____

_____

_____

_____

*Thank you for our legacy of faith and for the
new blessings you show us every day.*

DECEMBER 2

How do you determine how much to spend on
Christmas gifts for the various people on your list?

20___

20___

20___

Show us how to be good stewards of everything we have, Lord.

If money were no object, what would you buy for each other?

20___

_____

_____

_____

_____

20___

_____

_____

_____

_____

20___

_____

_____

_____

_____

"The servant brought out gold and silver jewelry and articles
of clothing and gave them to Rebekah; he also gave costly
gifts to her brother and to her mother." —GENESIS 24:53

Which Christmas decoration means the most to you?

20__ _____

_____

_____

_____

_____

20__ _____

_____

_____

_____

_____

20__ _____

_____

_____

_____

_____

Help us slow the busy pace of the season and
remember who and what really matters.

There's no gift like the gift of time. Whom can
you invest more time in the coming year?

20___

20___

20___

"A friend loves at all times, and a brother is born
for a time of adversity." —PROVERBS 17:17

DECEMBER 6

If you could travel anywhere this Christmas,
where would you like to go?

20___

20___

20___

Keep us safe as we travel, Lord.

What's a holiday song you love? What's
one you never want to hear again?

20___

20___

20___

What do you remember about your first date together?

20___ _____

_____

_____

_____

20___ _____

_____

_____

_____

20___ _____

_____

_____

_____

_____

Thank you for the memories you've placed in our hearts.

DECEMBER 9

You probably know a couple who's no longer together.
What can you learn from their relationship?

20___

20___

20___

"This is the message you heard from the beginning: We should love one another." —1 JOHN 3:11

What would you love to hear your kids (or a relative's kids) say to you? What do you think they would love to hear from you?

20___

20___

20___

What's something you'd text each other that
you feel awkward saying out loud?

20___ _____

_____

_____

_____

20___ _____

_____

_____

_____

20___ _____

_____

_____

_____

_____

Thank you for the ones who know us best, Lord.

DECEMBER 12

How would your lives be different if you'd had
a bigger (or smaller) family growing up?

20___

20___

20___

DECEMBER 13

How could you be more involved in your church? Are
there activities you should do less of next year?

20___ _____

_____

_____

_____

_____

20___ _____

_____

_____

_____

_____

20___ _____

_____

_____

_____

_____

Dear God, thank you for hardworking volunteers; may
we find ourselves numbered among them.

Think of a couple who's been married a long
time. What would you like to ask them?

20___

20___

20___

What one piece of advice would you give to
a couple who is just starting out?

20_ _

20_ _

20_ _

Has this year had a recurring theme,
something that makes it stand out?

20___

20___

20___

As the year draws to a close, thank you, Lord, for the
blessings and the lessons it has brought us.

DECEMBER 17

If you could choose a direction for next
year, how would you like to steer it?

20___ _____

_____

_____

_____

20___ _____

_____

_____

_____

20___ _____

_____

_____

_____

"He has made everything beautiful in its time. He has also set
eternity in the human heart; yet no one can fathom what God
has done from beginning to end." —ECCLESIASTES 3:11

Would you prefer to be way out on the edge or at the center of attention? Has that changed this past year?

20___

20___

20___

Show us how to appreciate the differences present in all of us.

DECEMBER 19

Think about last Christmas. Is there something you
want to be sure to do again? Is there something
you'd like to do differently this year?

20___

20___

20___

As we celebrate, as we enjoy being together, let us give you thanks, Father God.

DECEMBER 20

What I want for Christmas is...

20__ _____

_____

_____

_____

20__ _____

_____

_____

_____

20__ _____

_____

_____

_____

"On coming to the house, they saw the child with his mother Mary,
and they bowed down and worshiped him." —MATTHEW 2:11

Does the lack of sunshine affect your mood?
If so, what keeps your bells jingling?

20_ _ _____

20_ _ _____

20_ _ _____

What do you really enjoy about spending more
time together during the holidays?

20___ _____

_____

_____

_____

20___ _____

_____

_____

_____

20___ _____

_____

_____

_____

Help us grow in patience, Lord.

What's a secret blessing you could give someone this year?

20____
_____
_____
_____
_____

20____
_____
_____
_____
_____

20____
_____
_____
_____
_____

"When you give to the needy, do not let your left hand
know what your right hand is doing, so that your
giving may be in secret." —MATTHEW 6:3-4

What do you appreciate about your church's Christmas
Eve service? What would you change, if anything?

20__ __

20__ __

20__ __

*Thank you for the services that bring us closer
to each other and to you, Lord.*

Read the Luke 2 account of Jesus's birth. What
strikes you about it that hasn't before?

20__

_____

_____

_____

_____

_____

20__

_____

_____

_____

_____

_____

20__

_____

_____

_____

_____

_____

Thank you for Jesus, the reason for the season.

What makes for a perfect, cozy day at
home this holiday season?

20___ ___

20___ ___

20___ ___

We're so grateful for safe, warm, and happy homes. Thank you, Lord!

DECEMBER 27

Do you enjoy sleeping in, or is morning a productive time
for you? How has that worked out in your relationship?

20__ _____

_____

_____

_____

_____

20__ _____

_____

_____

_____

20__ _____

_____

_____

_____

_____

"It is good to praise the LORD and make music to your
name, O Most High, proclaiming your love in the morning
and your faithfulness at night." —PSALM 92:1-2

DECEMBER 28

In this season of miracles, who's been a miracle in your life?

20___

_____

_____

_____

_____

20___

_____

_____

_____

_____

20___

_____

_____

_____

_____

Thank you so much for the people you've placed in our
lives, Lord. Show us how to treasure them.

If you have kids or young family members with you right now, how can you make this time special for them?

20___

20___

20___

"These commandments that I give you today are to be on your hearts. Impress them on your children. Talk about them when you sit at home and when you walk along the road, when you lie down and when you get up." —DEUTERONOMY 6:6-7

DECEMBER 30

What burdens are on your mind regarding the upcoming year?
How can you help lighten those burdens for each other?

20___

20___

20___

Show us where we're tempted to get anxious and help us find peace.

DECEMBER 31

What do you enjoy about the way you
celebrate the start of a new year?

20___

20___

20___

"If anyone is in Christ, the new creation has come: The old
has gone, the new is here!" —2 CORINTHIANS 5:17

Cover design, hand-lettering, and illustration by Kristi Smith, Juicebox Designs

Question of the Day for Couples

Copyright © 2019 by Harvest House Publishers
Published by Harvest House Publishers
Eugene, Oregon 97408
www.harvesthousepublishers.com

ISBN 978-0-7369-7785-2 (pbk.)
ISBN 978-0-7369-8088-3 (exclusive edition)

Printed in China

19 20 21 22 23 24 25 26 27 / RDS-AR / 10 9 8 7 6 5 4 3 2 1